Grade 7 Aural
Intensive Exercise
(Singing, Cadence and Modulation)

(Based on ABRSM Grade 7 Aural Syllabus)

Regina Pratley

ISBN: 1984138510
ISBN-13: 978-1984138514

DEDICATION

Dedicated to you, who are frustrating about the aural part of your grade 7 instrument exam
and you, who want more exercise in the style of the real exam
and you, who want to get higher marks in the exam!

CONTENTS

Chapter 1
Part A: Singing from Memory

A glimpse at the exam:
In part A of the aural exam,
you need to sing or play from memory the lower part of a two-part phrase played twice by the examiner.
The examiner will play the key-chord and the starting note and then count in two bars.
If you choose to play, the examiner will also name the key-chord and the starting note,
as appropriate for your instrument.

Here are some exercise for you, key name and key chord are given at the start of each exercise:

Exercise 1
C major

Exercise 2
C major

Exercise 3
C major

Exercise 4
A minor

Moderato

Exercise 5
A minor

Allegretto

Exercise 6
A minor

Andante

Exercise 7
G major

Andantino

Exercise 8
G major

Allegro

Exercise 9
G major

Vivace

Exercise 10
E minor

Allegretto

Exercise 11
E minor

Andante

Exercise 12
E minor

Allegro

Exercise 13
F major

Moderato

Exercise 14
F major

Andante

Exercise 15
F major

Allegro

Exercise 16
D minor

Moderato

Exercise 17
D minor

Andante espressivo

Exercise 18
D minor

Andantino

Exercise 19
D major

Maestoso

Exercise 20
D major

Con brio

Exercise 21
D major

Moderato

Exercise 22
B minor

Andantino

Exercise 23
B minor

Andante

Exercise 24
B minor

Con moto

Exercise 25
B flat major

Allegro

Exercise 26
B flat major

Andantino

Exercise 27
B flat major

Andante

Exercise 28
G minor

Andantino

Exercise 29
G minor

Moderato

Exercise 30
G minor

Andante

Exercise 31
A major

Moderato

Exercise 32
A major

Exercise 33
A major

Exercise 34
F# minor

Exercise 35
F# minor

Exercise 36
F# minor

Moderato

Exercise 37
E flat major

Allegro

Exercise 38
E flat major

Allegretto

Exercise 39
E flat major

Con brio

Exercise 40
C minor

Adagio

Exercise 41
C minor

Andante

Exercise 42
C minor

Andantino

Chapter 2
Part B: Sight Singing

A glimpse at the exam:
In part B of the aural exam,
you need to sing the upper part of a two-part phrase from score.
The examiner will play the lower part of the phrase.
The phrase will be in major or minor key with up to 4 sharps or flats.
You may choose to sing from treble or bass clef. The examiner will name and play the key-chord and the
starting note and then give the pulse. You will have around 15 seconds to prepare.

Here are some exercise for treble clef singers,
key name and key chord are given at the start of each exercise:

Exercise 1
C major

Andante

Exercise 2
C major

Moderato

Exercise 3
A minor

Exercise 4
A minor

Exercise 5
A minor

Exercise 6
G major

Exercise 7
G major

Con brio

Exercise 8
G major

Cheerfully

Exercise 9
E minor

Andante

Exercise 10
E minor

Andantino

Exercise 11
F major

Grazioso

Exercise 12
F major

Moderato

Exercise 13
D minor

Slowly

Exercise 14
D minor

Allegretto

Exercise 15
D minor

Moderato

Exercise 16
D major

Allegro

Exercise 17
D major

Andante

Exercise 18
D major

Con moto

Exercise 19
B minor

Moderato

Exercise 20
B minor

Allegretto

Exercise 21
B flat major

Andantino

Exercise 22
B flat major

Slowly

Exercise 23
G minor

Delicato

Exercise 24
G minor

Mesto

Exercise 25
G minor

Andante espressivo

Exercise 26
A major

Moderato

Exercise 27
A major

Exercise 28
A major

Exercise 29
F# minor

Exercise 30
F# minor

Exercise 31
E flat major

Andante

Exercise 32
E flat major

Allegro

Exercise 33
C minor

Andantino

Exercise 34
C minor

Adagio

Exercise 35
C minor

Moderato

Exercise 36
E major

Andante

Exercise 37
E major

Con moto

Exercise 38
C# minor

Lento

Exercise 39
C# minor

Allegro

Exercise 40
C# minor

Andante

Exercise 41
A flat major

Moderato

Exercise 42
A flat major

Andante

Exercise 43
F minor

Triste

Exercise 44
F minor

Allegro moderato

Exercise 45
F minor

Poco adagio

And here are some exercise for bass clef singers:

Exercise 1
C major

Andante

Exercise 2
C major

Moderato

Exercise 3
A minor

Andante

Exercise 4
A minor

Adagio

Exercise 5
A minor

Allegretto

Exercise 6
G major

Moderato

Exercise 7
G major

Con brio

Exercise 8
G major

Cheerfully

Exercise 9
E minor

Andante

Exercise 10
E minor

Andantino

Exercise 11
F major

Grazioso

Exercise 12
F major

Moderato

Exercise 13
D minor

Slowly

Exercise 14
D minor

Allegretto

Exercise 15
D minor

Moderato

Exercise 16
D major

Allegro

Exercise 17
D major

Andante

Exercise 18
D major

Con moto

Exercise 19
B minor

Moderato

Exercise 20
B minor

Allegretto

Exercise 21
B flat major

Andantino

Exercise 22
B flat major

Slowly

Exercise 23
G minor

Delicato

Exercise 24
G minor

Mesto

Exercise 25
G minor

Andante espressivo

Exercise 26
A major

Moderato

Exercise 27
A major

Andantino

Exercise 28
A major

Allegretto

Exercise 29
F# minor

Exercise 30
F# minor

Exercise 31
E flat major

Exercise 32
E flat major

Exercise 33
C minor

Andantino

Exercise 34
C minor

Adagio

Exercise 35
C minor

Moderato

Exercise 36
E major

Andante

Exercise 37
E major

Exercise 38
C# minor

Exercise 39
C# minor

Exercise 40
C# minor

Exercise 41
A flat major

Moderato

Exercise 42
A flat major

Andante

Exercise 43
F minor

Triste

Exercise 44
F minor

Allegro moderato

Exercise 45
F minor

Poco adagio

Chapter 3
Part C: Cadence and Chords (Major)

A glimpse at the exam:
In part C, you have to identify the cadence
at the end of a phrase as perfect, imperfect or interrupted.
The examiner will name and play the key chord.
The phrase will be in a major or minor key and will be played twice by the examiner.

Afterwards, you have to identify the 2 chords that formed the above cadence.
The key chord will be given again. And then the examiner will play the 2 chords as a pair.
You may answer using technical names (tonic, subdominant, etc.), chord numbers (I, IV, etc.) or letter
names (C major, F major, etc.)

In this book, exercise in major and minor keys are separated
so that students can have a more focusing practice.
Key name and key chord are given at the start of each exercise.

Here are some hints on identifying cadence in major key:

Cadence	Hints	Chord progressions
Perfect	**End in tonic chord** (i.e. the key chord given by the examiner)	**V- I (dominant- tonic)** or **V⁷-I (dominant seventh- tonic)**
Imperfect	The last chord is in **major** quality, but it's **not** the **tonic chord** (key chord)	**I- V (tonic- dominant)** or **IV- V (subdominant- dominant)**
Interrupted	The last chord is in **minor** quality	**V- vi (dominant- submediant)** or **V⁷- vi (dominant seventh- submediant)**

Here are some exercise for you:

Exercise 1
C major

Maestoso

Exercise 2
C major

Allegro

Exercise 3
G major

Allegretto

Exercise 4
G major

Con moto

Exercise 5
F major

Moderato

Exercise 6
F major

Andantino

Exercise 7
D major

Andante

Exercise 8
D major

Andante

Exercise 9
B flat major

Moderato

Exercise 10
B flat major

Lively

Exercise 11
A major

Allegro moderato

Exercise 12
A major

Allegretto

Exercise 13
E flat major

Con moto

Exercise 14
E flat major

Allegro

Exercise 15
E major

Andante

Exercise 16
E major

Lively

Exercise 17
A flat major

Con moto

Exercise 18
A flat major

Moderato

Chapter 4
Part C: Cadence and Chords (Minor)

Here are some hints on identifying cadence in minor key:

Cadence	Hints	Chord progressions
Perfect	**End in tonic chord** (i.e. the key chord given by the examiner)	**V- i (dominant- tonic)** or **V⁷- i (dominant seventh- tonic)**
Imperfect	The quality of the last 2 chords must be **minor to major**	**i- V (tonic- dominant)** or **iv- V (subdominant- dominant)**
Interrupted	The quality of **the last 2 chords are major**	**V- VI (dominant- submediant)** or **V⁷- VI (dominant seventh- submediant)**

Here are some exercise for you:

Exercise 1
A minor

Exercise 2
A minor

Exercise 3
E minor

Exercise 4
E minor

Andante

Exercise 5
D minor

Vivace

Exercise 6
D minor

Allegro

Exercise 7
B minor

Alla marcia

Exercise 8
B minor

Andante

Exercise 9
G minor

Moderato

Exercise 10
G minor

Andante espressivo

Exercise 11
F# minor

Allegro

Exercise 12
F# minor

Andantino

Exercise 13
C minor

Moderato

Exercise 14
C minor

Waltz

Exercise 15
C# minor

Moderato

Exercise 16
C# minor

Andante

Exercise 17
F minor

Scherzando

Exercise 18
F minor

Andante

Chapter 5
Part C: Modulation

A glimpse at the exam:
In part C, you have to identify the modulation at the end of a passage.
The passage will begin in a major key.
The key name and the key chord will be given by the examiner.
The passage will be played once by the examiner.
You may answer using technical names (dominant/ subdominant/ relative minor)
or the letter name of the new key (e.g. D major/ F minor, etc.)

Here are some exercise for you, key name and key chord are given at the start of each exercise:

Exercise 1
C major

Lively

Exercise 2
C major

Moderato

Exercise 3
C major

Andante

Exercise 4
G major

Allegro

Exercise 5
G major

Moderato

Exercise 6
G major

Allegro

Exercise 7
F major

Allegretto

Exercise 8
F major

Andante

Exercise 9
F major

Cheerfully

Exercise 10
D major

Andante

Exercise 11
D major

Allegro

Exercise 12
D major

Moderato

Exercise 13
B flat major

Allegretto

Exercise 14
B flat major

Andante

Exercise 15
B flat major

Andantino

Exercise 16
A major

Exercise 17
A major

Exercise 18
A major

Exercise 19
E flat major

Exercise 20
E flat major

Presto

Exercise 21
E flat major

Andante

Exercise 22
E major

Andante

Exercise 23
E major

Andantino

Exercise 24
E major

Exercise 25
A flat major

Exercise 26
A flat major

Answer Keys

Chapter 3
Part C: Cadence (Major)
1. Perfect Cadence   V- I
2. Interrupted Cadence   V- vi
3. Imperfect Cadence   IV- V
4. Perfect Cadence   V7- I
5. Perfect Cadence   V- I
6. Imperfect Cadence   IV- V
7. Interrupted Cadence   V7- vi
8. Interrupted Cadence   V- vi
9. Imperfect Cadence   I- V
10. Perfect Cadence   V7- I
11. Interrupted Cadence   V7- vi
12. Imperfect Cadence   IV- V
13. Perfect Cadence   V7- I
14. Interrupted Cadence   V7- vi
15. Imperfect Cadence   I- V
16. Perfect Cadence   V7- I
17. Interrupted Cadence   V- vi
18. Imperfect Cadence   I- V

Chapter 4
Part C: Cadence (Minor)
1. Interrupted Cadence   V7-VI
2. Perfect Cadence   V7-i
3. Imperfect Cadence   i- V
4. Perfect Cadence   V7- i
5. Perfect Cadence   V- i
6. Imperfect Cadence   iv- V
7. Interrupted Cadence   V- VI
8. Imperfect Cadence   iv- V
9. Interrupted Cadence   V7- VI
10. Perfect Cadence   V- i
11. Imperfect Cadence   i- V
12. Imperfect Cadence   iv- V
13. Interrupted Cadence   V7- VI
14. Perfect Cadence   V- i
15. Interrupted Cadence   V7- VI
16. Imperfect Cadence   iv- V
17. Perfect Cadence   V- i
18. Interrupted Cadence   V- VI

Chapter 5
Part C: Modulation

1. Dominant (G major)
2. Subdominant (F major)
3. Relative minor (A minor)
4. Relative minor (E minor)
5. Dominant (D major)
6. Subdominant (C major)
7. Dominant (C major)
8. Relative minor (D minor)
9. Subdominant (B flat major)
10. Relative minor (B minor)
11. Subdominant (G major)
12. Dominant (A major)
13. Dominant (F major)
14. Relative minor (G minor)
15. Subdominant (E flat major)
16. Relative minor (F# minor)
17. Dominant (E major)
18. Subdominant (D major)
19. Dominant (B flat major)
20. Subdominant (A flat major)
21. Relative minor (C minor)
22. Relative minor (C# minor)
23. Dominant (B major)
24. Subdominant (A major)
25. Subdominant (D flat major)
26. Dominant (E flat major)

Notes

Printed in Great Britain
by Amazon

11782234R00036